PHOTOGRAPH 51

Anna Ziegler

PHOTOGRAPH 51

OBERON BOOKS
LONDON

WWW.OBERONBOOKS.COM

First published in 2015 by Oberon Books Ltd
521 Caledonian Road, London N7 9RH
Tel: +44 (0) 20 7607 3637 / Fax: +44 (0) 20 7607 3629
e-mail: info@oberonbooks.com
www.oberonbooks.com

Reprinted with revisions in 2018, 2020

A catalogue record for this book is available from the British Library.

PB ISBN: 9781783199358
E ISBN: 9781783199365

Cover design and photograph of Nicole Kidman by Dewynters

For Will, Elliot and Nathaniel, my balance

Acknowledgements

This play was developed with the generous assistance of the following organizations and individuals: Mary Resing and Active Cultures Theatre; William Carden, Graeme Gillis and The Ensemble Studio Theatre; Doron Weber and The Alfred P. Sloan Foundation; Andy Polk and The Cape Cod Theatre Project; Simon Levy, Aria Alpert and The Fountain Theatre; Evan Cabnet; Ari Roth, Shirley Serotsky and Theater J; Jerry Manning and The Seattle Repertory Theatre.

Special thanks go to Linsay Firman, Daniella Topol and Braden Abraham, whose singular visions of this play led to productions as different as they were enthralling.

The deepest gratitude to Nicole Kidman, Michael Grandage and James Bierman, who felt this story deserved a bigger stage and then made it happen, and so beautifully.

As always, thanks to my family – my parents, my brothers, my husband, my sons, and my grandfather, the incomparable Bobby Lewis.

And a final thanks to the real scientists behind the characters depicted here. Each opened his or her eyes in the darkness and brought something new out into the light. Lastly – it must be said – the incredible Rosalind Franklin's life lends itself to drama in part because it ended so tragically – would that this had not been the case.

Characters

ROSALIND FRANKLIN

a scientist in her 30s; she's brilliant, always on her toes, and doesn't suffer fools

MAURICE WILKINS

a scientist in his 30s or 40s; he's formal and polite, refined, restrained, gentle and wounded

RAY GOSLING

a scientist in his 20s; he's awkward, endearing, sweet, lacking in confidence

DON CASPAR

a scientist in his 20s or 30s; he's open, affable, humble and honest

JAMES WATSON

a scientist in his early 20s; he's all confidence, arrogance, hunger and drive

FRANCIS CRICK

a scientist in his 30s or 40s; he's very proper, not unkind, brash, a comedian philosopher, who enjoys being the center of attention

Setting

Many and various. The simpler the set, the more fluidly the action can move forward.

Note

This play is based on the story of the race to the double helix in England in the years between 1951 and 1953, but is a work of fiction. I have altered timelines, facts and events, and recreated characters for dramatic purposes.

Photograph 51 had its New York premiere at the Ensemble Studio Theatre (William Carden, Artistic Director), a production sponsored and developed by the Ensemble Studio Theatre/ Alfred P. Sloan Foundation Science & Technology Project where it opened on November 1, 2010. The director was Linsay Firman, the stage manager Danielle Buccino, the set designer Nick Francone, the costume designer Suzanne Chesney, the lighting designer Les Dickert, and the sound designer Shane Rettig. The cast was as follows:

ROSALIND FRANKLIN	Kristen Bush
MAURICE WILKINS	Kevin Collins
RAY GOSLING	David Gelles
DON CASPAR	Benjamin Pelteson
JAMES WATSON	Haskell King
FRANCIS CRICK	Jeremy Webb

Photograph 51 was subsequently produced by the Michael Grandage Company at the Noël Coward Theatre, West End, London, opening on September 14, 2015. The director was Michael Grandage, the stage manager Howard Jepson, the set and costume designer Christopher Oram, the lighting designer Neil Austin, and the sound designer Adam Cork. The cast was as follows:

ROSALIND FRANKLIN	Nicole Kidman
MAURICE WILKINS	Stephen Campbell Moore
RAY GOSLING	Joshua Silver
DON CASPAR	Patrick Kennedy
JAMES WATSON	Will Attenborough
FRANCIS CRICK	Edward Bennett

Photograph 51 was originally commissioned and produced by Active Cultures, the vernacular theatre of Maryland (Mary Resing, Director), opening on February 10, 2008.

This play is the winner of the 2008 STAGE International Script Competition and was developed, in part, through the University of California, Santa Barbara's STAGE Project by the Professional Artists Lab (Nancy Kawalek, Director) and the California NanoSystems Institute.

Certain things exist outside of time. It was ten years ago, it was this morning…It happened in the past and it was always happening. It happened every single minute of the day…

*

He felt like he was seeing greatness, like he was in the room watching Watson and Crick put the final touches on their model of DNA, or maybe he was seeing Rosalind Franklin with her magnificent X-rays. Wasn't it the girl, after all, who had actually found the key to life?

Ann Patchett, *Run*

As scientists understand very well, personality has always been an inseparable part of their styles of inquiry and a potent, if unacknowledged, factor in their results. Indeed, no art or popular entertainment is so carefully built as is science upon the individual talents, preferences and habits of its leaders.

Horace Judson, *The Eighth Day of Creation*

The lights rise on ROSALIND.

ROSALIND: This is what it was like. We made the invisible visible. We could see atoms, not only see them–manipulate them, move them around. We were so powerful. Our instruments felt like extensions of our own bodies. We could see everything, really see it – except, sometimes, what was right in front of us.

When I was a child I used to draw shapes. Shapes overlapping, like endless Venn diagrams. My parents said, "Rosalind, maybe you should draw people? Don't you want to draw our family? Our little dog?" I didn't. I drew patterns of the tiniest repeating structures. In my mind were patterns of the tiniest repeating structures.

WILKINS: It was a particularly cold winter in London. January 1951.

ROSALIND: And when I first got to use my father's camera, I went outside and found four leaves. I arranged them carefully, on the curb. But the photograph I took was not of leaves. You see, nothing is ever just one thing. This was the world, a map of rivers and mountain ranges in endless repetition. And when I told my father I wanted to become a scientist, he said, "Ah. I see."…Then he said "No."

WILKINS: And at the same time, in Paris–

WATSON: Not again, Wilkins. Really?

WILKINS: In Paris, Rosalind Franklin was saying her goodbyes.

WATSON: I promise it'll end the same way.

WILKINS: *(Ignoring him.)* There was a party for her at the Laboratoire Centrale. Everyone stayed late into the night, drinking and telling stories, entreating her not to leave.

CRICK: *(To the audience.)* But she'd just won a fellowship at King's College London and one didn't turn down a job at King's–especially since there was a chance she'd get to work in the field of genetics–

CASPAR: A field in which the possibilities were…well, they were endless. In which the promise of personal and professional fulfillment was tangible.

WILKINS: *(To CASPAR, sharply.)* What are you doing here?

GOSLING: So she wrote a…polite letter requesting the instruments she'd require:

ROSALIND: *(Writing the letter, cold and formal.)* I require an X-ray generating tube. And a camera specially made so that the temperature inside it can be carefully controlled. Otherwise, the solution will change during its exposure, and Dr. Wilkins you know as well as I do that that just won't do. Finally, if at all possible, I'd like to know when this order will be placed so that, if need be, I can request a few minor modifications. Yours sincerely, Dr. Rosalind Franklin.

WILKINS: Dear Miss Franklin, you are ever so…cordial. But I must warn you–we at King's are very serious. So serious, in fact, and intent on being at "the cutting edge" as they say, that we will be moving your research into another area entirely.

WILKINS and ROSALIND at King's together.

ROSALIND: I beg your pardon?

WILKINS: Yes, instead of proteins you will be working on deciphering the structure of DNA.

ROSALIND: Is that so.

WILKINS: You see, I recently took X-ray photos of DNA that came out remarkably well, showing that it is unmistakably crystalline in shape. Therefore it now seems evident that King's needs to push forward in determining, through crystallography, at which you are quite expert–

ROSALIND: Thank you. I am.

WILKINS: *(Thrown for a moment.)* …Yes. No one will argue with that. *(Beat.)* At any rate, we need to push forward in determining why it is that in the chromosome the numbers of purines and pyrimidines come in pairs. So that we can then determine how replication works. So that we can then determine–

ROSALIND: I know what you're talking about.

WILKINS: Yes, yes I suppose you do. Then I'll leap straight to the point. You will be assisting me in my study of the Signer DNA from Switzerland. Everyone wanted it and yet somehow Randall got it. The old rogue. I don't know how he did it…

ROSALIND: *(Icy.)* I don't think I heard you right.

WILKINS: You did! We have the Signer stock. Quite a coup really. When you think about it.

ROSALIND: But did you say *I'd* be assisting *you*?

WILKINS: Yes! …And my doctoral student, Ray Gosling, will assist *you.*

GOSLING: *(Putting out his hand, which ROSALIND ignores.)* Hello!

ROSALIND: But…Randall told me I'd be heading up the study. That I'd be in charge of my own work here. Surely, there's been some misunderstanding.

WILKINS: No. No misunderstanding. Circumstances changed. You see…we now feel that if we discover *this* structure–this structure–we could discover the way the world works, Miss Franklin. What some are calling "the secret of life." Can you imagine that?

ROSALIND: Dr. Wilkins, I will not be anyone's assistant.

Beat.

WILKINS: What was that?

ROSALIND: I don't like others to analyze *my* data, *my* work. I work best when I work alone. If, for whatever reason, I am forced into a different situation, I should feel that I came here under false pretenses.

WILKINS: I see… *(Giving this some thought.)* Then perhaps we could think of our work together as a kind of partnership. Surely that will suit you?

ROSALIND: I don't suppose it matters whether or not it suits me, does it?

She exits.

GOSLING: Well, that went well.

WATSON: See? She was meant to be Wilkins' *assistant,* and therein lay the problem. She misunderstood the terms. And after that, the rest was inevitable. The race lost right there. In a single moment.

WILKINS: No–nothing is inevitable.

CASPAR: She would never have left Paris to be someone's subordinate. She was quite clear with me about that.

CRICK: Well, that's not what we heard.

CASPAR: You heard what you wanted to hear. One of those specialties of human nature.

WILKINS: Is it really absolutely necessary that you be here too?

GOSLING: Anyway! We began. It was gray in London in January. We were working in a…well, it must be said, dank cellar in the Strand. There were no two ways about that.

ROSALIND, WILKINS and GOSLING are spread out in the lab, working.

ROSALIND: Could it be any gloomier here? As your *partner,* I might entreat you to find us a more hospitable working environment.

WILKINS: Labs are more nicely appointed in Paris, then?

ROSALIND: There's no comparison.

WILKINS: You know, not all of us felt we should leave England when she needed us most.

ROSALIND: Thank you, Dr. Wilkins, for your patriotic spirit. I can assure you, however, that I was doing much more for British society after the war by working on coal molecules in France than I would have had I been in London eating rationed food and parking my car on a site cleared by a bomb that used to be someone's home.

WILKINS: I was only joking–really.

GOSLING: *(Trying to lighten the situation.)* It's true–he's quite the jokester.

ROSALIND: And aren't you the same Wilkins who worked on the Manhattan Project in *California* during the war?

WILKINS: *(Proudly.)* For a few months' time, yes.

ROSALIND: Maybe you're aware of the fact that not a single female scientist from Britain was given a research position during wartime?

WILKINS: Is that so.

ROSALIND: I'll have you know that nuclear force is not something of which I approve.

WILKINS: Then I suppose it's good no one asked you to work on it.

ROSALIND: I beg your pardon?

WILKINS: *(Attempting to joke.)* At any rate, you lot never do seem to approve of it.

ROSALIND: I'm not sure I understand what you're driving at.

GOSLING: No, he–

WILKINS: All I meant was–the irony of...

ROSALIND: What irony?

WILKINS: *(Without apology.)* Just that...people...worked hard to...come up with these ways to save...well, the Jews, and then all you hear back from them is how they don't approve. It feels a little...

ROSALIND: You're absolutely right that the Jews should be in a more grateful frame of mind these days.

WILKINS: All right, Rosy.

ROSALIND: My name is Rosalind. But you can call me Miss Franklin. Everyone else does.

WILKINS: Fine.

ROSALIND: Of course I'd prefer Dr. Franklin but that doesn't seem to be done here, does it, Mr. Wilkins?

WILKINS: Dr. Wilkins.

ROSALIND: Dr. Wilkins, I don't joke. I take my work seriously as I trust you do too.

WILKINS: Of course I do.

Long beat.

GOSLING: How do you like that–it's nearly two already.

WILKINS: No need for constant updates on the time, Gosling. There's a clock right there that we can see perfectly well–

GOSLING: No…I was just saying, or, I mean, suggesting, that perhaps we might take our lunch?

ROSALIND: We've been having so much fun that the time has really flown, hasn't it, Dr. Wilkins?

WILKINS: Has it.

ROSALIND: So where shall we go? I'm famished, actually.

WILKINS starts to leave; he's off to lunch.

Dr. Wilkins?

WILKINS: *(Turning back.)* Hm?

Off her look.

Oh, I'd love to have lunch, but…

ROSALIND: But what?

WILKINS: *(Matter-of-fact.)* I eat in the senior common room.

ROSALIND: That's where we'll go then.

WILKINS: That's the thing.

ROSALIND: What's the *thing*?

WILKINS: It's for men only.

ROSALIND: Is that so.

WILKINS: It is.

Beat.

ROSALIND: Well go to it then.

WILKINS: If you're sure.

ROSALIND: Absolutely.

WILKINS: All right then.

GOSLING: *(To the audience.)* The next hour was…well, it wasn't what you'd traditionally think of as fun.

ROSALIND: It's absurd, isn't it? Archaic!

GOSLING: What is?

ROSALIND: Well, this business of the senior common room, of course.

GOSLING: I suppose. But…you can't worry about it.

ROSALIND: I can worry over whatever I choose to worry over, Mr. Gosling!

GOSLING: It's not like biophysicists have such great conversations at meals anyway. They tend just to talk about the work. They never take a break.

ROSALIND: But those are precisely the conversations I need to have. Scientists make discoveries over lunch.

GOSLING: If you say so.

ROSALIND: Can I ask you a question?

GOSLING: Of course.

ROSALIND: What's he like–Wilkins. You've worked for him for a few years, haven't you?

GOSLING: And now they've moved me along to you. The conveyer belt chugs along. But doctoral students are good people to work with. We're like liquids–we take the shape of the vessel into which we're poured.

ROSALIND: What do you mean by that?

GOSLING: That you don't have to worry about a thing: my allegiance will be to you. You're my advisor now.

ROSALIND: *(Taken aback.)* Well, good. I would have expected as much.

GOSLING: Wilkins is fine. Between you and me he's a bit of a stiff, but I'm sure you two will get along. He's easy enough to get along with. And he works hard. You know, no wife to go home to, no children. He devotes himself completely.

ROSALIND: So do I.

GOSLING: What does Mr. Franklin have to say about that?

ROSALIND: *(Archly.)* There is no Mr. Franklin. Unless, of course, you're referring to my father.

Beat.

GOSLING: No. I wasn't. I'm sorry. I really didn't mean to offend. I didn't mean to–

WILKINS entering, cutting GOSLING off.

ROSALIND: And how was your lunch, Dr. Wilkins?

WILKINS: Just fine. Thank you for asking.

ROSALIND: I'm glad that on my first day here you didn't take a break from your daily routine to accompany me somewhere I was permitted to dine.

WILKINS: Miss Franklin…Let me be clear about something: I was looking forward to your arrival here.

GOSLING: He truly was.

WILKINS: That's enough, Gosling.

GOSLING: But you talked about it all the time–how her chemistry and your theory would be a perfect marriage of–

ROSALIND: My chemistry and your theory? Are you suggesting I don't have theory, Dr. Wilkins?

WILKINS: Of course not.

ROSALIND: Good.

GOSLING: He was just fantasizing about a life free of all the menial tasks associated with biochemistry–

WILKINS: Gosling!

ROSALIND: Menial?

WILKINS: No! And all I wanted to say was that I don't like that things have got off to a…rocky start. I'd like to begin again.

Beat.

ROSALIND: All right.

WILKINS: All right?

WILKINS puts out his hand to shake, and she does grudgingly.

ROSALIND: I'm Dr. Rosalind Franklin. It's a pleasure to meet you.

WILKINS: It's a pleasure to meet you too.

ROSALIND: I've heard so much about you.

WILKINS: And I you.

GOSLING: Hi–I'm Ray Gosling. I'll be your doctoral student.

WILKINS: Unnecessary, Gosling.

ROSALIND: Yes, Gosling, *we've* already met.

WILKINS: May I ask you, Miss Franklin, what you're most looking forward to here at King's?

ROSALIND: I think, Dr. Wilkins, I'm looking forward to dispensing with these games at which point I can begin taking photographs of crystals of DNA. It wasn't what I came here to do but if we want to discover the secret of life as you put it, I'll do it with the cameras I choose from what's here and the sample from the Signer stock. You can use whatever's left and come reintroduce yourself to me whenever you'd like.

ROSALIND exits.

WILKINS: I see.

CASPAR: Did it really happen that way? Were you quite so…

WILKINS: I wasn't anything. I was perfectly fine…

To GOSLING.

A bit of a stiff perhaps, but otherwise…

GOSLING: Oh did you hear that bit?

WILKINS: *(Annoyed.)* Yes, I heard "that bit."

CRICK: Well, *I* don't think you're at all… You're not at all… well, all right you can be quite stiff, if you don't mind my saying.

WILKINS: *(Sarcastic.)* Why ever would I mind?

ROSALIND entering

ROSALIND: Good morning, Dr. Wilkins.

WILKINS: Good morning, Miss Franklin.

ROSALIND: Did you have a nice weekend?

WILKINS: It was fine, I suppose.

Beat.

How was yours?

ROSALIND: Fine.

WILKINS: Did you do anything interesting?

ROSALIND: Yesterday I went to the matinee of *The Winter's Tale* at the Phoenix. Peter Brook directed it.

WILKINS: That's funny.

ROSALIND: Why is that funny?

WILKINS: I almost went to see the very same performance. I was in the vicinity, walking, and I passed the Phoenix and I very nearly went in.

ROSALIND: It was sold out?

WILKINS: No. I never got that far.

ROSALIND: Then where's the coincidence?

WILKINS: It's just that…our paths so nearly crossed.

Beat.

Was it any good?

ROSALIND: Oh yes. Very.

WILKINS: The great difference, you know, between *The Winter's Tale* and the story on which it's based–Pandosto–is that in Shakespeare's version the heroine survives.

ROSALIND: John Gielgud played Leontes. He really was very good. Very lifelike. Very good. When Hermione died, even though it was his fault, I felt for him. I truly did.

WILKINS: And who played Hermione?

ROSALIND: I don't remember. She didn't stand out, I suppose.

WILKINS: My favorite part, you know, is Antigonus's dream.

ROSALIND: Why?

WILKINS: Because even though Hermione tells him to name her child Perdita, which of course means 'lost', she is instructing him to save her. To find her. Naming her lets her live.

Come, poor babe:

I have heard, but not believed–

ROSALIND: *The spirits o' the dead*

May walk again.

WILKINS: Did they do that bit well?

ROSALIND: Yes.

WILKINS: It can really take you away with it, don't you think? When it's done well. Make you forget yourself a little. Your regrets.

Beat.

ROSALIND: *(Quietly acceding.)* Yes. I suppose it can.

WILKINS: *(Finding his footing again.)* My grandfather committed a great number of Shakespeare's plays to memory.

ROSALIND: As did my father!

WILKINS: Really, in their entirety?

ROSALIND: Well, the good ones.

WILKINS: It's so damned impressive. I've always wished I could do the same.

ROSALIND: Then why don't you do it?

WILKINS: *(With levity.)* Oh I don't know. Laziness?

ROSALIND: *(Immediately unimpressed.)* Laziness?

WILKINS: Haven't you heard of it?

ROSALIND: I don't believe in it.

WILKINS: *(Realizing this is true.)*...No. I suppose not.

Beat.

ROSALIND: I'll leave you to it then.

WILKINS: But what are you planning to work on this morning?

ROSALIND: I'll be trying to get an image of DNA that isn't destroyed by the lack of humidity in the camera.

WILKINS: Hm. I suppose we need to fix that problem, don't we.

ROSALIND: *(Taking umbrage.)* Yes. I suppose *we* do.

Lights shift.

CASPAR: Dear Dr. Franklin.

GOSLING: Don Caspar was a doctoral student in biophysics at Yale. Unlike me, he was actually pretty close to getting his PhD. Not that I was so far off. Or, okay…I was. I don't know why it took me so incredibly long. My mother has her theories but we won't get into those.

CASPAR: My advisor, Simon Dewhurst, recommended I contact you since I'm considering doing the final stage of my doctoral research on the chemical makeup of coal molecules. You are, according to him, the world's expert on the subject. I gather you combine a theoretical and applied approach and this is precisely what I am hoping to do. So, I would be delighted…no…grateful if you would send me some of your scholarship on coal. X-ray images and published articles would be most appreciated.

ROSALIND: Dear Mr. Caspar: Thank you for your letter. Published articles are published and therefore you can access them just as well as I can. It might be possible, however, to send X-ray images so long as you assure me you know how to read them. I would prefer to avoid misinterpretations of my work cropping up all over New Haven. I should like to maintain the reputation your Dr. Dewhurst so kindly attributes to me.

CASPAR: Dear Dr. Franklin, I never received the images in the mail, even though I assured you I understood how to read them. Could you please re-send? It's been over a month and I'm anxious to finalize this section of my dissertation.

Beat.

Dear Dr. Franklin, I'm so sorry to write again, but I still haven't received the images. I'm afraid I've become a pest. Please forgive me. It would kill me to think you might think badly of me, as I'm such an admirer of your work.

ROSALIND: *(Offhanded.)* Dear Mr. Caspar, I trust you have now received the images?

CASPAR: Dear Dr. Franklin, I have indeed received the images. And I can't thank you enough. They've opened up for me…I mean, you've opened up for me a whole new…What I mean is, I've never seen anything like them. I could stare at them for hours and they still wouldn't reveal all of their secrets. Not that that means I can't read them. I can read them. I just mean that they're beautiful–these shapes within shapes, shapes overlapping, shapes that mean more than what they seem at first glance but are also beautiful simply for what they are. *(A new idea.)* I think one sees something new each time one looks at truly beautiful things.

ROSALIND: *(Formal.)* Thank you, Mr. Caspar. I'm pleased you received the images.

WILKINS: *(Unimpressed.)* One sees something new each time one looks at truly beautiful things?

CASPAR: Yes. I think so. And so did she.

GOSLING: *(To the audience.)* Sometimes she would get away from the lab. I'd arrive in the morning and no one would be there–

WILKINS: *(Hurt/indignant at being overlooked.)* Well, I was there.

GOSLING: And then the telephone would ring.

ROSALIND: *(On the telephone with GOSLING.)* I'm in Switzerland. Switzerland I said.

GOSLING: What? I can't hear you.

ROSALIND: I told you I was going hiking this week-end. I'm just going to stay an extra day.

GOSLING: Fine.

ROSALIND: Can you hear me?

GOSLING: She would just disappear sometimes. One day here and then gone–

WILKINS: Like a restless ghost.

ROSALIND: It's beautiful here, Gosling. You should have smelled the air at the summit; it was–

GOSLING: You have to speak up. I just can't–

ROSALIND: My head feels clear for the first time in ages and I've been doing some really wonderful thinking. I believe I've worked out how to fix the camera. And the Alps seem larger and yet somehow less overwhelming than they have in the past, as though their vastness was made for me, as though the more of something there is to climb, the further I'll get to go. It seems so obvious now. The mountains mean more than what they seem at first glance but are also beautiful simply for what they are… You know, I think one sees something new each time one looks at truly beautiful things.

GOSLING: Miss Franklin? Rosalind? Are you there?

WATSON: *(Unimpressed.)* But she wasn't there, was she. She was too busy snow-shoeing and…enjoying things like… nature and small woodland creatures.

CRICK: I mean, didn't she feel that something was at her back, a force greater than she was…

WATSON: You mean us?

CRICK: No. I mean fate.

WATSON: What's the difference?

WILKINS: And then she'd come back.

ROSALIND: Gosling, more to the left. I said the left.

GOSLING: I am moving it to the left.

ROSALIND: More, you have to move it more. We're simply not aligned.

ROSALIND moves into a beam of light.

GOSLING: Don't step there, Miss Franklin, please!

ROSALIND: Dammit.

GOSLING: You can't move through the beam like that.

ROSALIND: If I have to do everything myself, I will. I mean, don't you understand I will literally go mad if we don't get a better image soon. So let's get it done, Gosling. It's as simple as that.

GOSLING: *(Quietly.)* It doesn't have to be.

ROSALIND: What was that?

GOSLING: I said I'm here to help you. I just don't want to…

ROSALIND: What, Gosling? Don't want to what?

GOSLING: *(To the audience.)* I was going to say "endanger myself" but I didn't. I could have said, "put myself in harm's way," could have said that even though we didn't know it for sure yet, I could feel the way that beam cut through my flesh. Instead I said:

Yesterday's photographs *were* better, the best yet–did you see them?

ROSALIND: Of course I did.

GOSLING: There was a little crowd around them this morning, marveling at them, at the detail you captured.

ROSALIND: *(Feigning disinterest.)* Was there?

GOSLING: Absolutely. They were enthralled.

Beat.

It's quite gratifying, really. You should feel…

ROSALIND: But they need to be so much clearer, Gosling…If we're ever to find the structure.

GOSLING: I know.

ROSALIND: It's going to get to the heart of everything, Ray.

GOSLING: But you still need to sleep, occasionally. Don't you? Or don't you need any?

ROSALIND: We can call it a night, if you like.

GOSLING: You mean, why don't *I* call it a night?

ROSALIND: *(Smiling to herself.)* They were really enthralled, were they?

GOSLING: Like chickens clucking around a new bit of food.

ROSALIND: Go home, Ray.

GOSLING: So long as you promise not to…

ROSALIND: What?

GOSLING: *(Not brave enough to say what he wants to say.)*…Stay too late. So long as you promise not to stay too late.

ROSALIND: I promise.

GOSLING: You're lying.

ROSALIND: Yes.

CASPAR: *(To GOSLING.)* Did she really do that?

GOSLING: All the time.

CASPAR: And you didn't…

GOSLING: I couldn't…It was like speaking bad French to a French person who insists then on speaking in English just to show you you're not good enough to speak to her in her own language, that she can walk all over you in any language, anywhere.

CASPAR: She did know a lot of languages.

GOSLING: That's not what I meant–

CASPAR: I know.

WILKINS: *(Interrupting.)* Then there was the conference in Naples, spring 1951. And it was typical enough. Everyone pretended to be terribly interested in everyone else's work. My lecture was on the last day and the room was nearly empty. I showed a few slides, explained why we felt DNA was worth studying as opposed to protein, and then packed up my things. I was about to leave but then a young man with really very odd hair blocked my path.

WATSON: I'm Dr. Watson.

WILKINS: Hello, Watson. Can I help you?

WATSON: It's Dr. Watson, but no matter…The thing is, I was fascinated by your presentation.

WILKINS: Well good, thank you.

WATSON: It makes me think–more than ever–that the gene's the thing. I mean, we have to get to the bottom of it–discover how it replicates itself. And so we need its structure. Your slides convinced me that this can and should be done. That the shape is regular enough that it can be studied.

WILKINS: Yes. I believe it is.

WATSON: It's just incredibly exciting.

WILKINS: What is?

WATSON: To be born at the right time. There's an element of fate to it, don't you think? And I don't believe in fate.

WILKINS: You said your name is?

WATSON: *(All confidence and presumption.)* Watson. And I was wondering if maybe I could work with you on nucleic acid? At King's? I don't mean to be presumptuous…

WILKINS: That is a bit…presumptuous. Have we even met before?

WATSON: I'm twenty-two. I already have my doctorate. From Indiana University. I'm currently doing research in Copenhagen on the biochemistry of virus reproduction.

WILKINS: And?

WATSON: What I'm trying to say is: the photographs from your lab are brilliant. I'd like to learn crystallography.

WILKINS: I'm not even positive that I know what we're talking about.

Beat. A new tactic.

WATSON: *(Matter-of-factly.)* When I was five, my father told me religion was the enemy of progress, a tool used by the rich to give purpose to the lives of the poor.

WILKINS: A rather bold assertion to make to a five year old.

WATSON: He said the *worst* thing is that it eradicates curiosity, because it solves everything. So in my house there was no God. Which meant I needed to go looking for my own set of instructions for life.

WILKINS: *(Not sure where this is going.)* Okay…

WATSON: Which I happened to find in birds.

WILKINS: *(Unimpressed.)* In birds, did you say?

WATSON: My father would take me bird watching. In time, I learned to distinguish two different birds by the tiniest detail. I saw how the males would court the females, singing the most elaborate songs. Sometimes the female joins in and it's a duet. Sometimes he sings only for her.

WILKINS: I'm sorry, but I don't really see the relevance of–

WATSON: *(A little annoyed.)* I saw that the natural world is full of secrets–and no one, least of all me, likes knowing there's a secret without knowing what it is. So I decided I would crack them. Work them all out. The secrets, Maurice–I can call you Maurice, can't I?

WILKINS: Well, no–

WATSON: And the biggest one out there now? The biggest secret? The gene, of course. It's all I can think of. All I see. And I want in on it.

WILKINS: You do, do you.

WATSON: I've gotta get in the race, Wilkins.

WILKINS: What race are you referring to, Watson?

WATSON: For the structure of DNA, obviously.

WILKINS: There is no race.

WATSON: Linus Pauling's on it, out at Caltech.

WILKINS: Well, he doesn't have the sample I have. Or the photographs.

WATSON: Or the photographer.

WILKINS: That's right.

WILKINS shuts his briefcase and walks away.

WATSON: Was it the biggest mistake of his life?

Beat, then with glee.

Without question.

WILKINS: People assume I must feel it *was*–not taking him on, and becoming partners. After all, maybe the two of *us* would have...Maybe later *my* name would have... rolled off the tongue. Been the answer to questions in the occasional pub quiz. I don't know. What happened happened:

WATSON: After our conversation, I approached Lawrence Bragg at the Cavendish, who took me on immediately. I was partnered upon my arrival with a scientist named Francis Crick.

CRICK: Do you prefer Jim, or James? Jim sounds more American to me. Or how about Jimmy?

WATSON: How about I tell you and you don't have to keep guessing.

CRICK: I like that idea.

GOSLING: *(To the audience.)* As a child, already sure he wanted to become a scientist, Crick confessed to his mother that he worried everything would be discovered by the time he grew up. She assured him that this wasn't the case. And from that moment on, he was single-minded…Which is truly impressive. I mean, I don't think I've set my mind to something for more than five minutes in my entire life without wanting then to put the kettle on or to find that letter my brother wrote me three years ago from Wales or to try to remember the song that was playing in the dance hall when that girl walked in who looked like she might almost be willing to talk to me.

Lights shift. Back in the lab.

ROSALIND: Hello, Dr. Wilkins.

WILKINS: Hello Miss Franklin.

ROSALIND: And how was your conference?

WILKINS: I hear from Gosling you're spending some late nights here.

ROSALIND: *(Sharply.)* I'm just doing my work, Dr. Wilkins. Nothing more.

WILKINS: May I see it?

ROSALIND: What?

WILKINS: Your work.

ROSALIND: Why?

WILKINS: We're partners, aren't we, Miss Franklin?

Beat.

Aren't we?

ROSALIND: Yes we are.

WILKINS: So let's have it then.

ROSALIND: For one, I fixed the camera.

WILKINS: The humidity is no longer an issue?

ROSALIND: It's no longer an issue.

WILKINS: How did you do it?

ROSALIND: It was simple, really. I used salt solutions.

WILKINS: And the salt didn't spray the DNA?

ROSALIND: No it didn't. I assured you it wouldn't and it didn't.

WILKINS: Well, I'm very impressed.

ROSALIND: There's no need to condescend.

WILKINS: I wasn't. I am seriously impressed.

ROSALIND: But that's ridiculous. You shouldn't be. I used the simplest of chemist's techniques.

WILKINS: Whatever you did, it was wonderful!

ROSALIND: What's wrong with you, Dr. Wilkins? You look flushed.

WILKINS: I do feel a little warm.

ROSALIND: Maybe you should sit down.

WILKINS: Yes.

He sits, gazing at her. A long beat.

ROSALIND: *(Sharply, awkwardly.)* All right. That should do it. I'm sure you're ready now to get back to work.

WILKINS stands and stares at her, shocked. Lights shift.

WILKINS: But how can we get anything done if she's constantly making me feel as though I'm being impolite to her? No, worse–offensive.

GOSLING: I think she's just settling in.

WILKINS: Did you know Linus Pauling's on DNA now, Gosling?

GOSLING: I didn't.

WILKINS: As I said, we really must push forward.

GOSLING: And we will.

WILKINS: All I've been is kind to her.

GOSLING: *(Warmly.)* So maybe kindness isn't working.

WILKINS: Kindness always works with women, Gosling. I'm a trifle concerned for you if you didn't know that.

WILKINS picks up a box of chocolates and enters the lab where GOSLING and ROSALIND are working; her back is to him.

GOSLING: *(Noticing the chocolates.)* Dr. Wilkins, you shouldn't have.

WILKINS: Oh–no–they're for…

GOSLING: I know who they're for.

ROSALIND: *(Turning around.)* Yes, Wilkins, can I help you?

She notices the box.

What is that?

WILKINS: May I speak with you?

ROSALIND: About what?

WILKINS: Privately.

ROSALIND: Well, all right. But quickly.

She nods at GOSLING, who doesn't understand at first.

GOSLING: Oh, right.

He leaves. A beat.

ROSALIND: So?

WILKINS: I got you these.

He hands her the box.

ROSALIND: What are they?

WILKINS: Chocolates. *(Beat.)* I bought them for you.

ROSALIND: Why?

WILKINS: Why?

ROSALIND: Yes, why?

WILKINS: Oh. I suppose because I think things between us haven't got off on a good foot. On the right foot. I want to…I wanted to…

ROSALIND: We've already started again once, haven't we? How often will we have to do this?

WILKINS: It's just that…I mean, I'd like to…have an easier relationship with you.

ROSALIND: But we're not here to have a relationship, Dr. Wilkins.

WILKINS: *(Turning red.)* I didn't mean a relationship in the, well…I meant a working relationship. An easier partnership.

ROSALIND: Was your wife cold?

WILKINS: I beg your pardon?

ROSALIND: Was she cold?

WILKINS: I don't know what you're…to what you're referring…

ROSALIND: You do, I think. After all, how many wives have you had?

WILKINS: One.

ROSALIND: An American who refused to return with you to England after the birth of your son.

WILKINS: Yes.

ROSALIND: So was she cold?

WILKINS: She could be.

ROSALIND: And I'm not her. We're not married. You don't have to try to win me over. In fact, you shouldn't try to win me over because you won't succeed. I'm not that kind of person.

WILKINS: I'm just trying to…

ROSALIND: What?

WILKINS: Be your friend.

ROSALIND: I don't want to be your friend, Dr. Wilkins.

WILKINS: You don't?

ROSALIND: No.

Beat.

WILKINS: Well then. Enjoy the chocolates.

He exits; the lights shift.

CASPAR: Dear Dr. Franklin, I hope this isn't out of turn, but I wanted to let you know how immensely helpful your images have been. The work is going well. Incredibly well, actually. This morning I realized that for once I *didn't* feel plagued by lack of direction, by this persistent question about what to do with my life and whether I've made the right choices. I have made the right choices. I just love…I mean does the X-ray camera ever seem like it's just an extension of your own eye, as though you and you alone possess the superhuman powers that allow you to see into the heart of things? To understand the nature of the world as though it's a secret no one else is meant to know?…I do. And I think you do too.

ROSALIND: *(All formality.)* Dear Mr. Caspar: Thank you for your letter. And…Yes. I do share some of your…ways of thinking. It's nice to hear that one isn't alone.

GOSLING: And then…then Wilkins gave a lecture and referenced "his" DNA work.

WILKINS: I didn't say it quite like that.

GOSLING: He announced, to great applause, that all the X-ray patterns *he'd* made indicated a clear central x, a helix. And it wasn't pretty–the aftermath, I mean. Not the helix. The helix was…beautiful.

ROSALIND: *(Condescendingly.)* Flushed with pride, are we?

WILKINS: I beg your pardon?

ROSALIND: X-ray patterns *you* made?

WILKINS: It was just a manner of speaking. Everyone knows who's on the team, that there is a team.

ROSALIND: Well, I don't know which X-ray patterns you were looking at, but in the ones I took, it's certainly not clear that there is a helix.

WILKINS: It's like you're unwilling to see it.

ROSALIND: *(Calmly.)* Dr. Wilkins, I was told–before I came to King's–that I would be in charge of X-ray diffraction. Given that, and given the credit you seem bent on grabbing all for yourself, when you deserve none of it, I would suggest, and would certainly prefer, if you went back to optics and your microscopes. A field no one will begrudge you because no one really cares about it.

WILKINS: Why are you doing this?

ROSALIND: I simply don't understand why you would state something, why you would tell a crowd of people, no less, that something is true when it's not.

WILKINS: It might be true!

ROSALIND: It's self-aggrandizement at the cost of any kind of integrity.

WILKINS: You want our funding to continue, don't you? Don't you?

ROSALIND: I'm just not terribly impressed by you is the thing.

WILKINS: Oh?

ROSALIND: You're not…you're just not…you don't command my respect.

WILKINS: That's it.

ROSALIND: I agree. That's it.

WILKINS: No one has ever spoken to me in this way. And I don't deserve it.

ROSALIND: Neither do I!

They part in opposite directions.

GOSLING: Neither did I! Not that that mattered.

The lights shift. ROSALIND is studying two prints.

ROSALIND: Would you look at these, Gosling.

GOSLING peers at the print.

How do you like that? I mean, how do you like that?

GOSLING peers some more.

Well?

GOSLING: What?

ROSALIND: Just look at them, Ray! Jesus.

GOSLING: I see two different X-ray patterns.

ROSALIND: Yes.

GOSLING: One is much more diffuse than the other.

ROSALIND: Yes!

GOSLING: What?

ROSALIND: Don't you see? They're both DNA. It exists in two forms.

CASPAR: A form and B form. The hydrated, longer one was B, and the shorter, wider one, A…It turned out that, before, they'd been looking at one on top of the other, like…well, a man and woman making love, at that point when one body is indistinguishable from the other. It had made them virtually impossible to study. But now Rosalind had discovered how to separate man and woman, how to brush them off, get them out of bed and really see them, naked before her. This achievement alone secured her place in history.

WATSON: *(Scoffing.)* Her place in history?

CRICK: Her place in history??

CASPAR: Well, it should have.

GOSLING: And its significance wasn't lost on Wilkins.

ROSALIND and WILKINS work with GOSLING between them.

WILKINS: Could you please ask Miss Franklin if she would mind terribly if I were to work with her on the A and B forms of DNA. I have some new samples and I think we should collaborate.

GOSLING: Miss Franklin, Dr. Wilkins would like to know if you might consider–

ROSALIND: Please tell him that I will not collaborate and I don't appreciate his desire to infringe on my material.

GOSLING: She says she will not collaborate–

WILKINS: And why is that precisely?

ROSALIND: He knows perfectly well.

GOSLING: She says you know perfectly–

WILKINS: My lord, what's there to be so afraid of??

GOSLING: He says "my lord"–

ROSALIND: I'm not afraid of anything!

GOSLING: She says she's not afraid of anything!

ROSALIND: I mean, I simply will not have my data interpreted for me!

WILKINS: I've really had enough of this.

ROSALIND: I agree.

WILKINS: I mean, I can't take it anymore. What's more, your antipathy is distracting everyone in the lab.

ROSALIND: We'll work separately then. I'll take the A form. And you can have B.

WILKINS: Maybe *I'd* like A.

ROSALIND: Maurice, you're being ridiculous.

WILKINS: Fine. B it is.

CRICK: And so Rosalind did her work. Or tried to. Painstakingly. Paying attention to every detail. Every discrepancy.

WATSON: You see, she was suddenly just a few steps away from the structure. But Rosalind didn't hypothesize the way Crick and I did; she proved things, and proving things, as all scientists know, isn't…well for one thing it isn't fast.

ROSALIND: Either the structure is a big helix or a smaller helix consisting of several chains. The phosphates are also clearly on the outside, and not within.

GOSLING: Did you hear that Linus Pauling's working on DNA again?

ROSALIND: I didn't.

GOSLING: Well, he is.

ROSALIND: Good for him.

GOSLING: I think Wilkins wants to speed things up. Make a model. The others are making models, you know.

ROSALIND: If you'd like to take the day off and build a model, Ray, you're welcome to do so. I'd suggest a train, or an automobile. Those tend to reflect reality fairly well.

CRICK: *(To the audience.)* You see, to Rosalind, making a model was tantamount to negligence. She needed to do all the calculations first, to sit in a dimly lit room and do the maths. So what ended up happening was that she and Wilkins both sat in separate dimly lit rooms, doing maths. Unsurprisingly–

WATSON: Wilkins got lonely.

WILKINS: I wasn't at all lonely.

WATSON: And so he'd visit his old friend Francis Crick in Cambridge. A brilliant new scientist had just joined the lab there too: me.

CRICK: Another pint then?

WILKINS: Oh why not.

CRICK: Yes! Why not. This is practically a celebration! I don't think I've seen you in–what–months now? You've been neglecting me, Maurice.

WILKINS: I know…Tell me what you've been up to. Still on those hemoglobins, Francis?

CRICK: Oh, well, actually–

WATSON: *(Leaping in to change the subject.)* But we're so enjoying hearing about your work.

WATSON glares at CRICK to get him to join in.

CRICK: *(A bit reluctantly.)* It's true…we know all about our own work.

WATSON: There's no fun in that.

WILKINS: It's nice to be here; I must say.

CRICK: She's really that bad?

WILKINS: Worse.

WATSON: The Jews really can be very ornery.

WILKINS: You're telling me.

WATSON: Is she quite overweight?

WILKINS: Why do you ask?

CRICK: James is many things but subtle is not one of them. So you must forgive him, over and over and over again.

WATSON: You don't need to apologize for me, Francis–

CRICK: Oh but I do.

WATSON: All I asked is if–

CRICK: You see, he imagines that she's overweight. The kind of woman who barrels over you with the force of a train.

WATSON: Or a Mack truck.

WILKINS: No, she's not like that. No. She's like…she's like…

Lights on ROSALIND somewhere else on the stage; WILKINS gazes at her.

CASPAR: *(To the audience.)* To Watson and Crick, the shape of something suggested the most detailed analysis of its interior workings. As though, by looking at something you could determine how it came to be…how it gets through each day.

WATSON: Tell us more about these recent photographs.

WILKINS: Well, they're getting clearer. Every day I think I see more, and then I wonder if my mind's playing tricks on me.

WATSON: So you really think it's a helix?

CRICK: Jim–

WILKINS: The thing is, she's keeping me from my own work. And she has all the best equipment, not to mention the best samples. She's hoarding everything.

WATSON: It looks like a helix, Maurice?

WILKINS: What? Oh. Yes. A helix.

CRICK: *(Eliciting a "what are you doing??" glare from Watson.)* Perhaps you should build a model.

WATSON: Well, no need to be hasty about it.

WILKINS: It doesn't matter either way! She's opposed–completely–to models. She doesn't think there's any way they could reflect reality at this point. Mere pointless speculation.

CRICK: *(Trying to help, to nudge WILKINS.)*

But is speculation always pointless?

WILKINS: I think as far as Rosy is concerned.

WATSON: She doesn't sound particularly rosy to me.

CRICK: Does she know you all still call her that behind her back?

WILKINS: Are you joking? She'd have us skinned.

WATSON: I can't wait to meet her.

WILKINS: Oh trust me. You can wait.

GOSLING: He didn't have to wait long. That winter King's held a colloquium on nucleic acid structure. I was the… well, I made coffee at the colloquium. That was my contribution. It was November 1951.

ROSALIND stands in a spotlight, or it's possible that we just hear her lines–a recording, or she speaks from offstage. In this scene, WATSON and CRICK watch her, or watch a space that represents her. Their lines should run over some of hers; they're talking over her.

ROSALIND: As we all know, a nucleic acid is a *macromolecule* composed of chains of monomeric *nucleotides.* This nucleic acid, which I'll shorthand as DNA, exists in two forms. / Let's show that slide.

WATSON: *(To CRICK.)* I wonder how she would look if she took off her glasses and did something novel with her hair.

CRICK: You may be onto something, Watson.

ROSALIND: All right. There it is. / Look closely at it.

WATSON: I mean, she could possibly be attractive if she took even the mildest interest in her clothes. But appearances aside, she is not…engaging.

CRICK: I'll grant you that.

ROSALIND: If you examine it, you can see the transition from A form to B form / in this hydrated sample.

WATSON: When we shook hands, her handshake was far too firm. There's nothing gentle, nothing remotely tender about her. She's a cipher where a woman should be. That said, she's not fat.

GOSLING: So busy analyzing the speaker, they didn't hear what she was saying. That she stated quite clearly that:

ROSALIND: Based on these calculations, we can be sure that the phosphates exist on the *outside* of the molecule. There is no question that this is the case.

GOSLING: And when Watson and Crick made their model a week or so later, everyone at King's was invited up to see it–after all, it was based on *our* work.

WATSON: Wilkins, what do you make of it?

ROSALIND: Where's the water?

CRICK: It's nice to see you too, Miss Franklin.

ROSALIND: DNA absorbs at least ten times more water than that.

WATSON: Is that right?

ROSALIND: I don't see how a molecule, if it's as you've imagined it, could hold together.

CRICK: How so?

ROSALIND: The phosphates have to be on the outside. Furthermore, the X-ray data has not proven that the molecule is, indeed, helical.

WATSON: You just don't want to admit that it's right.

WILKINS: It's not right, Watson. It would never hold together. Not like that. Perhaps if you'd told me what you were working on a few weeks ago I could have helped you with it.

CRICK: All right, old boy–

WILKINS: But you didn't do that, did you? And why not? Because you knew perfectly well it wasn't yours to ask about.

WATSON: Maurice–

CRICK: Be quiet, Jim. He's right–we should have told him.

WATSON: Why? It's a free country, isn't it?

CRICK: England? No, not in the slightest.

WATSON: Even if the model *is* wrong–I don't really see what the big deal is.

WILKINS: Then perhaps you should return to *your* country, where theft and burglary are upheld as virtues. In fact, it's how America came to be, isn't it? In Britain we don't actually believe in turning our sinners into saints.

WATSON: Hey, if you're angry with George Washington, don't take it out on me. I'm just trying to do some science here.

ROSALIND: You call that science?

WILKINS: Well you're not trying in the right way…And you're too young. And your hair…needs attention!

WATSON: I'm not too young.

CRICK: For my part I quite like his hair! I think it's got character!

CASPAR: It was a disaster. An embarrassment. The model, I mean. The Cavendish ordered Watson and Crick to stop working on DNA.

WILKINS: An oddly satisfying disaster, wouldn't you say, Ray?

GOSLING: I would, Dr. Wilkins. It was oddly satisfying.

CRICK: What bastards those King's boys can be, can't they? The way they condescended to us.

WATSON: Boys and *girl*.

CRICK: Right. I don't know how he puts up with her. They make quite a pair. I mean I love him dearly, I do, but even at university, Wilkins could be a patronizing prat.

WATSON: Oh come on. We'd be gloating too. If it'd been the reverse.

CRICK: It will be, one day. There's not a chance I'm going back to hemoglobin diffraction patterns.

WATSON: I don't blame you.

Lights shift. ROSALIND is on the telephone.

ROSALIND: You really don't have to worry about me, mother. I'm just fine. I always have been and nothing is different now…

Well, tell father the work is slow-going but…

Of course he's busy, so am I…

Yes: I am managing to sleep…

No. I'm not too lonely.

From offstage.

GOSLING: Miss Franklin!

ROSALIND: I've got to go. Yes. Friday night. Goodbye.

GOSLING: Miss Franklin!

She hangs up. GOSLING appears.

ROSALIND: What is it?

GOSLING: You just have to see it. It's sort of…well, amazing.

ROSALIND: Show me.

He shows her. She studies it for a long time.

ROSALIND: Gosling.

GOSLING: It's incredible, isn't it?

ROSALIND: How do you like that. How do you like that…I've never seen anything like it.

CASPAR: Photograph 51.

WATSON: Photograph 51.

GOSLING: It's certainly a helix. The B form is certainly a helix.

A beat.

ROSALIND: The B form certainly *looks to be* a helix.

GOSLING: Looks to be?

ROSALIND: *(To the audience.)* As a girl, I prided myself on always being right. Because I *was* always right. I drove my family near mad proposing games to play that I'd win every time. Scrabble. Ludo. Hide and Seek outside until the lamplighter appeared on his bicycle and our mother called us in, out of the dusk. Eventually and unsurprisingly I lost my opponents. And when I was at university, and it was becoming as clear to my parents as it always had been for me that I would pursue science, I left Cambridge to meet my father for a hiking weekend. Atop a mountain in the Lake District, when I was eighteen-years old, he said to me, "Rosalind, if you go forward with this life… you must never be wrong. In one instance, you could lose all you've achieved." But I didn't think this would be a problem. I was meticulous and I enjoyed being meticulous because I enjoyed being right. But it was in that moment that, without realizing it, a kind of fear set in, a dread around the edges of my convictions, like a hovering dusk no lamplighter ever truly dispels.

She looks again at the photograph, intently.

CASPAR: And she stood there, staring at the photograph, as though she were looking in a mirror but was suddenly unrecognizable to herself.

CRICK: *(Searchingly.)* Did any chimes go off in her head? Was there any singing?

WATSON: And then.

She opens a drawer and files it away.

WATSON: *(Shocked.)* She put it away.

GOSLING: Shouldn't we show it to Wilkins?

ROSALIND: Don't you want to celebrate, Gosling? We should celebrate.

WILKINS entering.

WILKINS: Celebrate what? I see no cause for celebration.

ROSALIND: You can have a little fun, can't you, Maurice? After all, we know how you like your games and jokes and things.

WILKINS: Do I?

ROSALIND: Why don't you give us a little speech.

WILKINS: I beg your pardon?

ROSALIND: Go on then.

WILKINS: A speech? About what?

ROSALIND: Be creative, Maurice. You can do that. Come up with something out of thin air. Can't you?…I don't know. Why don't you tell us about the fondest moment in your scientific career.

WILKINS: The fondest moment.

ROSALIND: Ray, does it seem he's just repeating after me?

GOSLING: Oh, um.

WILKINS: What is it precisely you want me to do?

ROSALIND: Just do *something*. Maurice. Something. You never commit to anything and it torments me.

WILKINS: Does it.

ROSALIND: Yes. I can't abide it.

GOSLING: I think Dr. Wilkins is just trying to…

ROSALIND: Oh, come on, Ray. Whose side are you on?

GOSLING: *(Directing the first phrase to ROSALIND and the second to WILKINS in quick, seamless succession.)* I'm not on a side. I'm not on a side.

WILKINS: You're behaving a bit like a banshee, Miss Franklin.

ROSALIND: Just celebrate with us.

WILKINS: But what are we celebrating??

GOSLING: It's amazing, really–

ROSALIND: Have some faith in me. There is something to celebrate. Take a leap of faith.

WILKINS: *(Bitterly.)* As though you would ever do that.

He chuckles, drily.

I mean, my God, can you even hear yourself? The irony?

ROSALIND: *(Slowly.)* I take a leap of faith every day, Maurice, just by walking through that door in the morning. I take a leap of faith that it'll all be worth it, that it will all ultimately mean something.

WILKINS: I don't know what you're talking about.

ROSALIND: No, you wouldn't.

WILKINS: You know, you really are unspeakably difficult. I've never encountered a woman with such temerity–

ROSALIND: Well perhaps it's that you haven't encountered very many women.

WILKINS: As you well know I was married!

ROSALIND: And maybe that's over and done with for a reason.

WILKINS: Oh, no. No. I refuse to get into this with you–

GOSLING: Dr. Wilkins–

WILKINS: *(Bitter and sarcastic and self-pitying, a dam bursting.)* No. I refuse to disclose the depths of my wife's cruelties to you. The lengths she took to keep me from our son; the words she said that repeat over and over in my head, like an infernal radio show that will never end. I will not get into it. I am not that kind of man. Perhaps you want to work with someone different. Someone who can happily remain in high dudgeon with you day in and day out. Well, I'm sorry–I am not that person. I'm sorry! Life is and has always been unfair. *That* is its enduring hallmark.

ROSALIND: Maurice–

WILKINS: A leap of faith. It's almost funny…Because *you* would never. No–it all has to be solved and re-solved.

There can be no room for error. No room for...humanity, really. That's what you leave out of *your* equations, Miss Franklin.

He leaves.

GOSLING: That night I slipped Wilkins the photograph. I did think it was his right to see it. I knew it was the best photograph we had.

CASPAR: Dr. Franklin, I graduated today!! As of this morning, I was still a student, and a mere few hours later, I'm not. I feel like one of my own X-ray exposures, one that took ages to set up and wasn't at all promising, but managed to yield something. A little something. Really, I can't believe it. Neither could my parents. They kept saying "Don, we thought you'd never finish." But they were happy. And...I was happy–am happy–and I just felt like telling you that I owe all of this to you. And I was wondering...do you think...I mean, is there any chance I could come work with you–for you–at King's? It would be a great honor. Maybe there's a fellowship I could look into?

ROSALIND: Dear *Dr.* Caspar, my most heartfelt congratulations. I'm sure you realize how important semantics are. This title that's now been conferred on you...It means windows have been flung wide, letting in the cold night air, that streetlamps will blink on as you walk past them. In 1945, when I got my doctorate, I thought those letters you've now acquired would have the same value for me, but of course you and I well know this is not the case. I'm not complaining about it. One can't focus on such things. And I don't.

CASPAR: You are so remarkable, Dr. Franklin. I really hope you don't mind my saying: you are so remarkable. I don't know how you exist in the environment in which you find yourself.

ROSALIND: I just do my work, Dr. Caspar. I've realized the best thing is just to do one's work and not worry so much about anything else. It doesn't matter anyway.

WATSON: But it does matter! It did matter. You can't be in the race and ignore it at the same time! That's where she went wrong.

WILKINS: You told her she was remarkable?

CASPAR: I did.

CRICK: And what is a race anyway? And who wins? If life is the ultimate race to the finish line, then really we don't *want* to win it. Shouldn't *want* to win it. Should we?

WATSON: I don't know what you're talking about. Sometimes you didn't make sense, Francis, and I had to pretend to understand what you were saying. I usually attributed it to a British thing, some guilty remnant of an imperialist past back to haunt you.

CRICK: Or maybe the race is for something else entirely. Maybe none of us really knew what we were searching for. What we wanted. Maybe success is as illusory and elusive as…well, Rosalind was to us. Maybe it exists only in our conception of it, and then always just out of reach, like Tantalus with his hovering grapes.

WATSON: See? Gobble-de-gook. It's amazing we got on so well for so long.

CRICK: *(Sarcastic.)* It is amazing.

Then, softening. The tension breaks and they smile at each other.

WATSON: In January 1953 we got our hands on a report Pauling had written about nucleic acid structure. It was wrong; he was wrong about the phosphates, but the simple fact of his writing it meant he was working on it in earnest, which meant he would get it.

CRICK: We all knew it was just a matter of time and not much time at that. So Watson went to London. He didn't tell me why, but I had a feeling.

WATSON bursts into ROSALIND's office.

WATSON: Good morning, good morning, lovely Rosalind.

ROSALIND: What are you doing here?

WATSON: It's nice to see you too.

ROSALIND: You could knock.

WATSON: Do you know what I have with me?

ROSALIND: How would I know?

WATSON: Pauling's manuscript.

ROSALIND: All right.

WATSON: All right?

ROSALIND: Look, I really was about to–

WATSON: Pauling is going to be publicly humiliated in two weeks when this gets published and you don't even want to see it?

ROSALIND: Why would I want to see it?

WATSON: To gloat, for one. You should see Bragg–he's walking on water these days; *(Impersonating Bragg.)* "Linus isn't going to beat me this time!" See, Pauling made some of the same mistakes Crick and I made. He's proposing a triple-stranded helix with the phosphates on the inside.

ROSALIND: That's what this rush to publish does. It means our publications are littered with ridiculous mistakes.

WATSON: Do you think DNA is a helix?

ROSALIND: I'm happy to arrange a time to sit down with you and discuss my findings but right now is not possible, unfortunately.

WATSON: Maurice says you're anti-helical.

ROSALIND: Maurice has no business saying who or what I am.

WATSON: So you think it is helical?

ROSALIND: I think it might be.

WATSON: Are you sure you're interpreting your data correctly?

ROSALIND: What did you just say?

WATSON: How much theory do you have?

A hair of a beat.

ROSALIND: Why are you here, Jim?

WATSON: *(Holding up PAULING's manuscript.)* To share.

ROSALIND: Oh, really?

Beat.

WATSON: I don't know. I thought you'd be interested in the manuscript. I thought…

ROSALIND: Yes?

WATSON: I thought we could talk.

ROSALIND: But you've never shown any interest in doing that before. Which leads me to believe that you're here to insult me. That or you're not aware of the fact that you're insulting me, which is, perhaps, worse. Do you think that if you demoralize me I won't get it done?

WATSON: Get what done?

ROSALIND: The work, Jim.

WATSON: I think you'll get it done. Or…I think you might get it done. But to do that, you have to compensate for the things you're lacking. And maybe I could do that.

ROSALIND: Do what?

WATSON: Help you.

ROSALIND: Really, if you wouldn't mind leaving–

WATSON: What I mean is, if you had theory you might understand how these "anti-helical" features in the A form are really distortions. That what you're seeing is, in fact, a helix. Because I really think it is one, Rosalind. I have this feeling that's divorced from reason. That I can't explain.

It's deeper than…I mean, if I've known anything for sure in my life, this is it.

ROSALIND: You must sleep so easily. With that kind of certainty.

WATSON: No. I don't sleep.

Beat.

There's too much to think about. You know there is. It overwhelms you. I can see that. So share your research with me. I mean, you're not going to get it on your own.

ROSALIND: Get out.

WATSON: Be reasonable, Rosalind.

ROSALIND: Get out of my lab!

WATSON: There's no need to get so upset–

ROSALIND: I'm not upset! I'm not upset. I'm…I'm…What I am is none of your concern. Just go.

WATSON: Why won't you even consider that–

ROSALIND rushes at him.

What's this all about?

ROSALIND: Out!

WATSON: Okay, okay.

He leaves.

ROSALIND: And stay out.

CASPAR: Down the hall, Watson was with Wilkins. Or Wilkins was with Watson. If it weren't in poor taste, they'd have been holding hands.

WILKINS: Don't be absurd.

CASPAR: I wasn't.

WATSON: She really is a right old hag, isn't she? I mean, the way she lunged at me. I really thought I might get hit.

WILKINS: A complete disaster. Did it to me once. All I was doing was trying to be congenial.

WATSON: Me too!

WILKINS: She takes everything so seriously.

WATSON: One needs to be more lighthearted sometimes. Every now and then at least.

WILKINS: I know.

WATSON: I mean, I can't believe this is what you've had to put up with. It's really more than anyone should be asked to do.

WILKINS: It really is.

WATSON: It is.

WILKINS: And it's all such a shame.

WATSON: What is?

WILKINS: That we're not actually partners. I suppose I ruined that before it even began.

WATSON: How could you have ruined it?

WILKINS: I was unfriendly, I suppose.

WATSON: *(Lying.)* Come on. You're one of the…friendliest men I know.

WILKINS: I know! I mean, I am pretty friendly. I've never offended anyone else.

WATSON: She must be crazy.

WILKINS: Maybe she is. Or maybe…

WATSON: What?

WILKINS: I don't know.

WATSON: Well, you're better off without her. Why collaborate with someone with whom it's impossible to get along?

WILKINS: The work, for one! I mean, you should see some of her…

He looks through a file in a drawer and pulls out a photograph.

This photograph she took of B, for instance.

WATSON: What photograph?

WILKINS: This one.

He hands it to WATSON, who studies it for a long time.

WATSON: I need to…

WILKINS: What?

WATSON: Go. I need to go.

WILKINS: Just like that?

WATSON is out the door.

James?

CASPAR: In *The Double Helix*, Watson later wrote "The instant I saw the picture my mouth fell open and my pulse began to race." It was Photograph 51.

WILKINS: You can't leave–just like that. James!

GOSLING: On the train back to Cambridge, he sketched the image in the margin of a newspaper. He stared at it. He stared at it some more. When the train pulled in, he stopped for a moment to notice two warblers perched atop a station lamppost; he was sure he heard their song as he ran like a wild man down the rainy streets–and then he arrived.

CRICK: What is it?

WATSON: The Nobel.

CRICK: What?

WATSON: The answer.

CRICK: What's the answer?

WATSON: It's a double helix. I saw it.

CRICK: Where?

WATSON: At King's. And we have to build another model. Right now. We have to start right now. We've got it, Francis. It's ours. They're sitting on it and they don't know it. It's ours. This is how we're gonna get to replication.

CRICK: But I don't quite understand.

WATSON: There's no time to understand. We just have to start.

CRICK: Well, let me at least finish this cup of tea. It's really such a lovely cup of tea –

WATSON: Francis!

CRICK: Oh, all right.

WILKINS: But that's not how it happened. I didn't just give him the photograph. He asked for it.

WATSON: No. I don't think so. You offered it up, like a leg of lamb we'd share for dinner.

WILKINS: I didn't.

GOSLING: And that same week–

WILKINS: *(Unhappily.)* Don Caspar arrived.

GOSLING: Shortly after getting his doctorate, Dr. Caspar was awarded a fellowship with us at King's. Apparently, one of the scientists here had gone to bat for him, so to speak. I can't imagine who it was.

The lights shift. WILKINS shepherds CASPAR into the lab.

WILKINS: And this is Miss Franklin.

CASPAR: You're Dr. Franklin?

ROSALIND: That's me.

CASPAR: Well, hello.

An awkward beat. WILKINS looks on, stunned.

It's funny…I imagined you differently.

ROSALIND: How did you imagine me?

CRICK: He didn't say–he couldn't say–that he'd imagined her dowdier. A woman whose exterior mirrored her seriousness.

CASPAR: Oh, just fairer maybe. Blonde.

ROSALIND: You thought I was blonde?

CASPAR: I don't know. Yes.

ROSALIND: You knew I was Jewish, though?

CASPAR: Yes. So am I.

ROSALIND: That will make two of us at King's.

CASPAR: I have left the States, haven't I.

ROSALIND: Yes. I suppose you have…And how was your journey?

WILKINS: His journey was fine–so, shall we?

CASPAR: It was fine. A little tiring.

ROSALIND: Yes–it must have been.

Beat.

CASPAR: It's strange to meet someone with whom one has–

ROSALIND: We should get to work then, shouldn't we?

WILKINS: Yes. I think work is the reason why we're all here, isn't it? Isn't it, Miss Franklin.

ROSALIND: It certainly is Dr. Wilkins.

GOSLING: Four days later Crick invited Wilkins for Sunday lunch in Cambridge. He found, when he arrived –

CRICK: I hope you don't mind that I invited Watson too.

WILKINS: No, of course not.

CRICK: What can I get you to drink? Odile is making a roast but it won't be ready for an hour or so.

WILKINS: Anything is fine. Whiskey?

CRICK: Whiskey it is.

CRICK exits.

WATSON: So how has it been lately with you-know-who?

WILKINS: Don't ask.

WATSON: She's working hard?

WILKINS: Same as always…

WATSON: People never change, do they.

WILKINS: No…And I wonder sometimes if perhaps I shouldn't move–you know, to the countryside. I can't really…That is to say, I haven't met anyone in London. Have you met anyone out here? I mean…I suppose I mean…women? Do you meet women?

CRICK returns with a drink.

CRICK: One whiskey.

WATSON: I have met a few women here. Sure.

CRICK: "Met" being the operative word. They take one look at him and then…how would one describe it…I suppose then there's a brief period of whispering after which time they end up leaving the pub because one turns out to have left her hat at home or some such nonsense. No, it's more likely James would solve the secret of life than bed a woman.

WATSON: Now why d'you say that? It's just none of the women here happen to appreciate my sophisticated charms.

WILKINS: Francis, do you remember Margaret Ramsay?

CRICK: You think I could forget Margaret Ramsay?

WILKINS: *(To WATSON.)* She was–

CRICK: One of the very few women in science at Cambridge. And he was absolutely smitten by her. And then one night they were sitting at opposite ends of his room, talking about the typical things one talked about, I suppose–and out of nowhere he tells her he's in love with her. The poor sod doesn't take her out, get a few drinks in her and kiss her. No he tells her he's fallen for her and then continues to sit there, waiting for some verbal reciprocation of his love.

WATSON: And what happened?

WILKINS: After a very long silence, she stood, said goodbye and left.

CRICK: See, women expect men to fall upon them like unrestrained beasts. Despite their murmurings to the contrary, they want to feel that you can't keep your hands off them. Maurice has never understood that.

WILKINS: I suppose what I'm wondering is…how do you and Odile…how does it work so well?

WATSON: It works because she doesn't know that he ogles every other woman who crosses his path.

CRICK: I don't! I mean, give me some credit. Sometimes I do much more than ogle.

WILKINS: But you love her?

WATSON: What is this? Twenty Questions?

CRICK: Of course I love her. I mean, honestly I don't know what I'd do without her. I can't even imagine that life. And as soon as we have the money, we're going to have gads of children…

WATSON: *(In horror.)* God, how many is that?

CRICK: Well, at least one.

He laughs but WILKINS looks away, sad.

CRICK: *(Studying WILKINS.)*

What is it, Maurice? Is something wrong?

Beat.

WILKINS: Oh, it's…I don't know. It's just that I'm starting to think there might come a point in life after which one can't really begin again.

WATSON: That's right. It's called birth. After that point, what's done is done. Which leads us nicely to a discussion of genes. So shall we discuss how the work is going?

WILKINS: *(With sarcasm.)* Yes, the work, the work. That is the important thing, isn't it?

WATSON: Do tell us what our little ray of sunshine is keeping busy with these days.

CRICK: *(Actually worried.)* Wilkins, old boy. Are you sure you're quite all right?

WATSON: Anything new on her docket? If you don't mind sharing, that is.

WILKINS: I honestly couldn't give two damns. I'm happy to tell you all I can remember.

WATSON: Well–good. Isn't that good, Crick?

CRICK: *(Reluctantly.)* Yes–it's good.

Beat. And a decision to go along with the change of topic.

WILKINS: So let's see…She's writing a paper at the minute. She might never finish it. The woman writes so slowly to begin with and lately she's been a bit distracted. Infuriating, really.

WATSON: What's it on then?

WILKINS: Her recent photographs, I'm sure. As you saw, they were the best yet.

WATSON: *(Tossed off.)* Yes. They were good. Very good.

And is she building a model?

WILKINS: Starting to entertain the idea. Which is actually something.

WATSON: Is she? I didn't know that. Francis, did you know that?

CRICK: I didn't know that, Jim.

WILKINS: She has so much information now she can no longer completely avoid it.

WATSON: What kind of model would she make?

WILKINS: One of B. It turns out A is no longer viable on its own. So essentially A *and* B have become hers. I'm not quite sure how that happened, but it happened. And yes, a model may come out of it. Someday.

CRICK: Oh, well good.

WATSON: That's terrific for her. *(Beat.)* We wish her well.

CRICK: Yes.

WILKINS: *(Shocked.)* You do??

WATSON: Of course.

CRICK: But how would you feel, Maurice, if…

WILKINS: What?

CRICK: I mean…what it is I mean to say is–

WATSON: He wonders if you'd be opposed to our trying. One more time. To get at the thing.

WILKINS: You want to build another model?

CRICK: Would that be all right with you?

WATSON: We wanted to ask you first. This time. Since it really is your…thing.

GOSLING: They neglected to mention that they'd already begun.

CRICK: You really should get to it yourself, old boy. You can do one too.

WATSON: It's a super idea. You do one too.

WILKINS: I can't do one. Not with Rosy around. It's her territory, her materials…

CRICK: So that's grand. You'll do it if Rosy ever leaves.

WATSON: Yes, grand! She's bound to go sometime, after all.

CRICK: And we'll get started on ours, so long as you give us the go-ahead.

WILKINS: I can't tell you what to do. I just…

WATSON: Yes?

WILKINS: I didn't know you were interested is all. In doing it yourselves. Not again. Not after what happened last time around. I mean, weren't you sufficiently embarrassed?

WATSON: Maurice, if I hid out after every embarrassment, I'd probably never be able to leave my room.

CRICK: And his room is an embarrassment. Utterly filthy. Why do you think he's here all the time?

WATSON: Odile's roasts aren't bad.

CRICK: You take that back. They're superb.

WATSON: Almost as tender as her thighs.

CRICK: Okay, that's enough.

WILKINS: Look, if I'd known you were going to do another, I wouldn't have…

CRICK: What, Maurice?

WILKINS: Said so much, I suppose. Or shown you…

GOSLING: Then things moved quickly. Quickly especially by the standards of a PhD student for whom everything moves slowly.

CASPAR: Watson and Crick got hold of the paper Rosalind had written. It was confidential.

CRICK: It wasn't confidential. Another scientist at Cambridge gave it to us after it was circulated to a committee over which he was presiding.

WILKINS: Well it wasn't published, that's for sure. And it included her latest calculations, confirmation that the B-form was helical, and the diameter of that helix. Information that became critical to your work.

WATSON: I'm sure we would have gotten there sooner or later, even without it.

WILKINS: So would we have done, with the benefit of your work. You had ours but we didn't have yours!

WATSON: There was no "we" where you were concerned. That was the problem.

GOSLING: Anyway, it doesn't matter how they got the paper, only that they got it.

CASPAR: And that Rosalind didn't know she should be in a hurry. Neither of us knew.

CASPAR is leaning over a microscope and ROSALIND tries to squeeze by him.

ROSALIND: Would you excuse me, Dr. Casp–

She brushes against him, just a little.

Oh I'm sorry.

CASPAR: *(Straightening.)* It's fine.

ROSALIND: I was just...

CASPAR: It's fine, Rosalind.

Beat.

ROSALIND: *(Taking offense.)* What's happened? You got your degree and somehow I lost mine?

CASPAR: I'm sorry–*Dr.* Franklin...It's just.

ROSALIND: What?

CASPAR: I like your name...Rosalind...Rosy.

ROSALIND: Why?

CASPAR: It's warm. It makes me think about coming inside to a fire after a walk in the bitter cold.

WILKINS: *(To the audience.)* Only an American could come up with such a line.

ROSALIND: But I'm not warm. No one thinks I'm warm. Ask anyone–

CASPAR: Listen...

ROSALIND: Yes?

CASPAR: Would you have dinner with me?

ROSALIND: Dinner??

CASPAR: No–not like…Just dinner…Something really casual.

ROSALIND: I don't think you understand that nothing in Britain is casual. No–everything here is filled with meaning no one will name or indulge. It's why I much preferred Paris.

CASPAR: But I would think it must have been very hard to be in Paris.

ROSALIND: Why's that?

CASPAR: I don't know. After the war. It must not have been too friendly to…

ROSALIND: Oh. Yes. But…you just have to get by, don't you? That's all one can do. You can't constantly be thinking about that…or I imagine it would destroy you.

CASPAR: It would. I'm certain it would.

Beat.

Have dinner with me.

Beat.

ROSALIND: I'm afraid there just isn't time, Dr. Caspar.

CASPAR: For dinner?

ROSALIND: Right.

GOSLING: In the meantime, Watson and Crick were working at breakneck speed.

CASPAR: After looking at Rosalind's report, they made a conclusion she had yet to draw: that DNA consisted of *two* chains running in opposite directions, a pair of endless spirals that work together but will never meet.

CRICK: Which will lead us to how it replicates, Watson. To how it all works.

...Do you know what this means?

WATSON: Yes. I mean, no.

CRICK: It means large homes in the countryside without leaky radiators. It means suits tailored to fit. It means my mother will stop politely asking why I didn't go into law, or medicine, and whether I have any regrets about the way my life has turned out...

WATSON: It means textbook publishers will call to make sure they have the correct spelling of our names.

CRICK: Yes! And you can choose any woman as your wife. And my wife will look at me differently.

WATSON: It means there will always be the means to keep doing this. Forever.

CRICK: We're almost there, Watson. We're so close.

GOSLING: Mid-February. Watson and Crick were all of a sudden being very friendly. They invited everyone to Cambridge–well, everyone except me–and then acted... strangely cheerful.

CRICK: Rosalind! So good to see you! Come in, come in–here, let me take your coat.

WATSON: You're looking particularly lovely today, particularly vibrant–

ROSALIND: Hello Jim. Francis. *(Beat.)* Maurice.

CRICK: And you must be Dr. Caspar.

CASPAR: Please–call me Don.

ROSALIND: Now what was so important that we come all the way here?

CRICK: Just the pleasure of your company, Miss Franklin, on a lovely winter's day. Nothing more.

WATSON: Why not wait out the winter doldrums together? By a warm fire, maybe, sipping the finest Cambridge has to offer.

ROSALIND: You'd be silly to waste a day like this indoors. And I certainly won't, not after being cooped up on the train all morning. Will you come with me to the garden… Don?

CASPAR: Of course…Rosalind.

WILKINS watches her take CASPAR's arm; the two exit together.

WILKINS: She's different.

WATSON: Not to me. Still the same old–

CRICK: Come now. Let's be kind.

WILKINS: *I've* always been kind to her! I've been nothing but kind!

He leaves them standing there.

CRICK: Oh.

WATSON: What was *that*?

CRICK: Ohhhhhhhhh.

WATSON: What??

CRICK: Don't you see?

WATSON: See what?

CRICK: Sometimes you can be so blind, Jim.

WATSON: I can be blind? That's a funny notion.

CRICK: He's in love with her.

WATSON: In love with who?

Beat.

No!!

CRICK: Undeniably.

WATSON: That's quite a theory, Francis. But do you have any proof?

CRICK: That's not the way we work, now. Is it.

ROSALIND and CASPAR come back inside. WILKINS is watching them.

ROSALIND: Francis–Dr. Casp–I mean, Don–just had the most fascinating idea–

WATSON: Oh yes? About what exactly? About helices, or?

ROSALIND: He was proposing that isomorphous replacement could be used with the Tobacco Mosaic Virus.

WILKINS: It's not so novel.

CRICK: No, it's a first class idea.

WATSON: So you'd put atoms of–

CASPAR: Lead, or maybe mercury–something heavy–

CRICK: Into the virus protein to see what the difference would be between the X-ray patterns. The X-ray with the atoms and the one without. That would determine the structure. It's very clever.

CASPAR: Soon enough we'll be making a model, right, Rosy?

WILKINS: She doesn't like being called Rosy.

An awkward pause.

ROSALIND: *(Quietly.)* I don't mind it.

WILKINS: And she doesn't like making models!

Awkward silence.

WATSON: But are you thinking of making one?

CRICK breaks in to stop WATSON from going on.

CRICK: And how much longer will you be in London, Caspar?

CASPAR: Not very much longer, I'm afraid. This fellowship is just a couple more months.

CRICK: Shame.

CASPAR: It is.

They all look at ROSALIND.

ROSALIND: Yes. *(Beat.)* Shame.

WILKINS: *(With unconcealed glee.)* Quite a shame. Yes.

WATSON: Wilkins, you old rogue.

WILKINS: What?

WATSON: Francis, I do believe you're right.

WILKINS: Right about what?

CRICK: Let's move into the sitting room, shall we? Jim, you go and help Odile bring out our new tea set and then we'll sit and have a nice cup.

WATSON: Why should I help her? She's *your* wife.

CRICK: Just go.

Lights shift.

CASPAR: But don't be fooled. She was not distracted by me. Rosalind? No. She continued to work slowly and methodically, and in increasing isolation.

GOSLING: Can I get you anything? A cup of tea at least?

ROSALIND: Gosling, if I were to tell you that it seemed to me the A form of DNA is *not* helical, what would you say?

GOSLING: I'd say you're testing me.

ROSALIND: How so.

GOSLING: Because if the A form is not helical, then neither can the B form be helical, and yet we are confident that it is.

ROSALIND: Yes.

GOSLING: So you were testing me.

ROSALIND: You always need to rule out the wrong answer, Ray. Don't forget that.

GOSLING: So then what's the right answer?

ROSALIND: What is the right answer.

GOSLING: Are you asking me?

ROSALIND: Do you know it?

GOSLING: No.

ROSALIND: Then I'm not asking.

CASPAR: Watson and Crick struggled with how the four bases fit into the picture. Did they pair up? Work together? Or were they distinct from each other?

WATSON: You can't be tired. Are you really tired?

CRICK: No. I'm wide awake. I'm just feigning fatigue to keep you on your toes.

WATSON: Are you kidding? I can't tell if you're kidding.

CRICK: I can't tell either.

GOSLING: February the 23rd.

ROSALIND is studying prints of the A and B forms. She holds them very far away from her face and then very close.

ROSALIND: Gosling! Can you come here, Gosling.

GOSLING: What is it?

ROSALIND: What are you doing over there, playing solitaire?

GOSLING: No, I was just–

ROSALIND: What do you think this is? Nursery school? I mean, we have work to do.

GOSLING: But you haven't been wanting my help–

ROSALIND: Please just stand here, will you. *(Beat.)* No–that's too close. Still a little further. I need you to be standing further away so I can think.

She picks up the photograph again, studies it.

Yes. Both the A and B form are helical. They have to be.

GOSLING: Two steps away from the solution. Two steps away. She just didn't know it.

WILKINS entering.

WILKINS: It's late. Why don't you go home.

ROSALIND: I'm fine.

WILKINS: Fine.

He begins to leave. She is staring at Photograph 51.

You're staring. I can tell you're doing nothing more than staring. Go home.

ROSALIND: No.

WILKINS: Or let me look at it.

He goes towards her.

Is it the bases? Are you thinking about the bases?

ROSALIND: I think I'm thinking about how I've come to the end of thinking. How there's nothing left.

WILKINS: You're exhausted.

ROSALIND: Not exhausted. Blank.

WILKINS: This rarely happens to you.

ROSALIND: It never happens.

WILKINS: Never?

Beat.

You think if you gave an inch, we'd all take a mile, is that it?

ROSALIND: *(Quietly.)* It's true, isn't it?

WILKINS: No. I don't think so.

ROSALIND: Then you too have come to the end of thought. You should go home, Maurice.

WILKINS: I could…

ROSALIND: What?

WILKINS: We could talk it through. It might help.

A long beat. She stares at WILKINS.

GOSLING: For a moment, everything stopped. Different ways our lives could go hovered in the air around us.

A long beat.

ROSALIND: You know, I think I *am* going to call it a night. I haven't been home before midnight for a fortnight and really what's the point of being here and not getting anywhere?

She stands abruptly.

GOSLING: And then there was only one way everything would go.

ROSALIND: Goodnight, Maurice.

She exits.

WILKINS: Goodnight.

GOSLING: February the 28th, 1953. A barmaid made her way through the Cambridge snow to open the Eagle Pub for the day. Watson and Crick were holed up like birds in a cage that was about to become…the world.

WATSON: They must pair off. The hydrogen bonds form between the pairs.

CRICK: Adenine always goes with thymine; cytosine with guanine.

WATSON: Whenever there's one on the DNA chain, there's always the other.

CRICK: Yes!

WILKINS: Like a team. A successful team.

GOSLING: And in the meantime, in a quiet Italian restaurant overlooking the Thames, where waiters stay out of people's way, Rosalind wondered if she was on a date. She couldn't be sure. She'd never been on one before.

ROSALIND and CASPAR sit at a table together. It's the end of the meal.

CASPAR: I'm glad you didn't change your mind. You know, I really thought you were going to change your mind. I hope I didn't take up too much of your time.

ROSALIND: My time.

CASPAR: Right.

ROSALIND: To be honest I'm not sure anymore how terribly valuable my time is…Or maybe I haven't been…allotting it to the right things. I don't know.

CASPAR: You don't know?

ROSALIND: Well, I…

CASPAR: You're serious.

ROSALIND: I'm sorry–I shouldn't have said anything.

CASPAR: Haven't you heard the story about the woman physicist who had to sneak into Princeton's lab in the middle of the night to use the cyclotron? And you probably know women aren't even permitted into Harvard's physics building.

ROSALIND: Yes. I know that.

CASPAR: And yet here *you* are, doing this amazing…no, groundbreaking work. And still you aren't sure you're allotting your time correctly? I can't think of a better allotment of anyone's time.

ROSALIND: I don't know.

CASPAR: Well, I do.

A breath.

ROSALIND: Should we get some tea then?

CASPAR: Rosalind…I have a confession. You might not like it.

ROSALIND: What?

CASPAR: I hate tea. I hate it. I mean, I really hate it. I can't even pretend to like it.

ROSALIND: Oh. Well, that is pretty bad. I think I'm rethinking everything I ever thought about you.

CASPAR: *(A genuine question.)* What did you think about me?

Beat. Awkward. Then, ROSALIND considers it.

ROSALIND: *(Honestly, openly.)* I thought…you seemed balanced.

CASPAR: If by balance you mean always *about* to take a horrible misstep and have it all come crashing down around me, then maybe…

ROSALIND: No…See, I've never had a balance.

Beat.

CASPAR: No?

ROSALIND: No.

CASPAR: But you've been happy.

A long beat–she is taken aback.

ROSALIND: Of course.

Beat.

Of course. Otherwise, why would I have…

CASPAR: Why would you have what?

ROSALIND: Continued on, I guess, in this way.

CASPAR: Right. You wouldn't have.

ROSALIND: Right.

CASPAR: You know, I have this theory…I think the things we want but can't have are probably the things that define us…And I've spent more time than I'd like to admit coming to this pretty simple conclusion so I hope you don't think it's completely ridiculous. But…I guess I'm talking about…I don't know…yearning?

ROSALIND: Yearning?

CASPAR: I mean…what do you want, Rosalind?

ROSALIND: So many things: to wake up without feeling the weight of the day pressing down, to fall asleep more easily, without wondering what it is that's keeping me awake, to eat more greens and also beetroot, to be kissed, to feel important, to learn how to be okay being with other people, and also how to be alone. To be a child again, held up and admired, the world full of endless future. To see my father look at me with uncomplicated pride. To be kissed. To feel every day what it would be to stand at the summit of a mountain in Wales, or Switzerland, or America, looking out over the world on a late afternoon with this man sitting across from me. Or to feel it once.

GOSLING: But instead she said:

ROSALIND: *(Sadly.)* I don't know.

CASPAR takes her hand.

CRICK: It's two strands. The bases go in the middle and the phosphates on the outside. It has to be.

WATSON: And we match the larger base with the smaller one.

They step back and look at the model they've created. Silence.

WATSON: Crick.

CRICK: Wait. Don't say anything.

WATSON holds up his sketch of Photograph 51; they look from sketch to model and back again.

CASPAR: Is this okay?

GOSLING: There's no science that can explain it. Loneliness.

ROSALIND looks down at her hand in his. The moment of possibility lingers. Then a strange look comes over her face.

CASPAR: Rosalind?

She clutches her stomach.

WATSON: It works, Francis. It works.

A very long beat.

CRICK: It's…

WATSON: I can't believe it.

CRICK: It's life unfolding, right in front of us.

ROSALIND doubles over in her chair, and gasps.

CASPAR: Rosalind?

WILKINS: It's the loneliest pursuit in the world. Science. Because there either are answers or there aren't. There either is a landscape that stretches before you or there isn't. And when there isn't, when you're left in the darkness of an empty city at night, you have only yourself.

CASPAR: I'll get you help. I'll bring you somewhere.

ROSALIND: A doctor.

CASPAR: Yes.

ROSALIND: Thank you.

CASPAR: Please don't thank me.

ROSALIND: Don't worry–I won't do it again. It wasn't easy for me.

Lights shift.

WILKINS: When they said they had something to show me, I had a feeling. All the way there on the train, the world seemed to move very quickly, as though passing me by.

He sees the model.

CRICK: Well?

WATSON: Say something, Wilkins.

ROSALIND: *(To the audience.)* I have two tumors. Twin tumors. Twins scampering around my body on tricycles, dropping handfuls of dirt as they go…For a moment I think of naming one Watson and the other Crick, but no, I tell myself: Rosalind, dispel the thought. *(Beat.)* No. I have ovarian cancer. A tumor in each ovary, one the size of a tennis ball, and the other a croquet ball, and they are indeed an efficient pair.

WATSON: You're really just going to stand there gaping? After all this?

CRICK: Let's have something at least. Come on. Give us something.

WILKINS: *(Resolutely.)* I think you're a couple of old rogues but you may well have something. I think it's a very exciting notion and who the hell got it isn't what matters.

WATSON: *(Matter-of-factly.)* An exciting notion? It's the secret of life, Wilkins.

WILKINS: *(Sadly.)* But is it? Is it *really*, Jim?

CASPAR: Rosalind, listen to me.

ROSALIND: Why? I'm not sure there is much else one could choose to see on those X-rays.

CASPAR: I'm going to find another hospital.

ROSALIND: Just go home, Don. I'm fine here.

CASPAR: How could you possibly think I'd leave you here all alone?

ROSALIND: But why would you stay?

CASPAR: Because I like you.

ROSALIND: *(Sadly; this isn't possibly enough.)* You like me.

He exits. The lights shift.

WILKINS: Dear Miss Franklin.

No.

Rosalind.

No.

Dear Dr. Franklin: I was so sorry to hear about your illness. I'm sure you'll come out on the other side of it, however, and be back at King's in no time. Really, you haven't missed much. Things have been exceptionally dull around here. The equipment is getting dusty from disuse; it's been raining nonstop, of course; Watson and Crick discovered the secret of life. My teeth hurt in the mornings, just after I wake up. Dr. Randall sends his regards. We all miss you.

No.

We trust you'll soon be well.

Yours, Maurice Wilkins.

Lights shift.

WATSON: *(Holding up the copy of 'Nature'.)* Can you believe it, Crick? I mean, can you really believe it?

CRICK: I can't, I can't.

WATSON: Why do you seem so tired? I can't sit still. I'm energized. I want to take on everything now. The world. Everything. Women. You know.

CRICK: And you will.

WATSON: Crick?

CRICK: You will…I'm just tired, I think.

WATSON: But wasn't it worth it? Now we'll never be forgotten.

CRICK: Never.

WATSON: That's right.

CRICK: Never forgotten.

WATSON: Francis?

CRICK: Truly all I ever wanted was to support my family, to do science, to make some small difference in the world.

WATSON: Is it really so awful that you ended up making a big difference instead?

CRICK: Odile has taken the guest room as her own. She moved her things into it slowly, gradually, over the last few months. She was clever. It was only when nothing was left that I realized she was gone.

Lights shift. ROSALIND sees WILKINS in her office.

ROSALIND: Maurice, what are you doing here? Why on earth are you sitting in my office in the dark?

WILKINS: Oh–I'm so sorry; I thought you were still…

ROSALIND: *(Matter-of-factly.)* I escaped.

WILKINS: You–?

ROSALIND: I don't intend to spend any more time in that hospital. If I'm going to be in a dank, disgusting little room, I may as well be here, where I might even get some work done before I die.

WILKINS: Please don't say that.

ROSALIND: Why not? It's not pleasant? It makes you think about your own life? The inevitability of your own death?

WILKINS: Yes. All of those things.

ROSALIND: Well, no one can protect you from those.

WILKINS: No. No I suppose not.

ROSALIND: We lose. In the end, we lose. The work is never finished and in the meantime our bodies wind down, tick slower, sputter out.

WILKINS: Like grandfather clocks.

ROSALIND: Well this has been a pleasant conversation.

WILKINS: Rosalind, I…

Beat.

ROSALIND: When I was fifteen, my family went on holiday to Norway. One morning, we woke at four and started up Storgalten…Mother couldn't stop complaining–it was too early, and too cold–until she looked around, that is. Because there we were, in the middle of a cloud. And we walked through it for what felt like an eternity, and there was no one else and there was no earth, no complicated history, no war about to unfold, just us, walking through this particular morning, watching the day begin.

At the time I told my father that I was moved by the natural beauty of our world: clouds–frozen crystals of ice suspended in the air, evaporating just before they hit the ground.

My father looked at me in a new way. He said yes that was true, but really we were seeing God–my father, who never believed. A man of science through and through. And when the sun rose, and the cloud lifted, we walked out onto the glacier, and he wept.

Beat.

WILKINS: You know…I've never felt the two have to be at odds.

ROSALIND: And yet they are intrinsically, unavoidably at odds.

Beat. They look at each other; something passes between them.

ROSALIND: So they really got it, did they? Our friends.

WILKINS: Yes.

ROSALIND: And is the model…is it just beautiful?

WILKINS: *(With real feeling.)* Yes.

ROSALIND: Well. We were close, weren't we? By god, we were close.

WILKINS: But we lost.

ROSALIND: Lost? No…We all won. The world won, didn't it?

WILKINS: But aren't you at all…

ROSALIND: Yes, but…It's not that they got it first…It really isn't…It's that I didn't see it. I wish I'd been able to see it.

WILKINS: I suspect you didn't allow yourself to see it…

ROSALIND: No, but with a little more time, I like to think I would have.

WILKINS: A few more days, even.

ROSALIND: So then why didn't I get those days? Who decided I shouldn't get those days? Didn't I deserve them?

Beat.

I mean, if I'd only…

GOSLING: Been more careful around the beam.

WATSON: Collaborated.

CRICK: Been more open, less wary. Less self-protective.

CASPAR: Or more wary, more self-protective.

WATSON: Been a better scientist.

CASPAR: Been willing to take more risks, make models, go forward without the certainty of proof.

CRICK: Been friendlier.

GOSLING: Or born at another time.

CRICK: Or born a man.

ROSALIND: But you'll see. The work never ends. Next month I'm going to go to a conference in Leeds with one of my colleagues from Paris. We're going to drive there, stop off at some Norman churches along the way.

WILKINS: Churches?

ROSALIND: I do love the shapes of things, you know. I love them even before they mean something.

GOSLING: But she never went to Leeds. Rosalind was thirty-seven when she died. It was a particularly cold April that year; there was frost on the trees in London; the Alps stayed snow-covered well into June.

WILKINS: No, no, no…I won't have it.

GOSLING: Eulogies about her focused on her single-minded devotion to work, the progress she made in her work, the lasting contributions she made through her work.

WILKINS: *(To GOSLING.)* Stop that! I said: stop that right now.

GOSLING: I can't. It's what happened.

CASPAR: It's the tricky thing about time, and memory. I tell my grandchildren: whole worlds of things we wish had happened are as real in our heads as what actually did occur.

WILKINS: Stop that right now. We start again. At the beginning. This instant.

CRICK: Come on, old boy, don't you think enough is enough?

WILKINS: Not until we've gotten it right! We start again.

WATSON: You've gotta be kidding me, Wilkins. I mean, you won. We won. Your name on the Nobel Prize. Remember that part? For God's sakes: this was the finest moment in your life.

WILKINS: No. It wasn't.

He turns to ROSALIND.

We start again. Just us this time.

WILKINS: *(Pleading with her, while the others exit.)* Please…You see, I need…

ROSALIND: *(Gently.)* What is it you need, Maurice?

WILKINS: There's something I need to tell you…It's important.

ROSALIND: Then tell me.

Beat.

WILKINS: I saw you. The day you went to see *The Winter's Tale* at the Phoenix.

ROSALIND: This is what you needed to tell me?

WILKINS: And I wanted to join you. I got in the queue to buy a ticket.

ROSALIND: All right, so what happened?

WILKINS: It's not what happened…It's what could happen. Now.

ROSALIND: What are you talking about, Maurice?

WILKINS: January, 1951. This time, I attend the play. And I see you across the theater.

He looks to her. She remains still, unmoved.

WILKINS: This time, we make eye contact. And afterwards, we meet in the back. By the bar.

She doesn't move.

WILKINS: This time I say, "did you enjoy the performance?"

She stares at him. Says nothing.

WILKINS: "Gielgud is excellent, don't you think?"

Beat.

ROSALIND: Yes, very lifelike. Very good.

WILKINS: And the incredible thing is we're both there, watching him. Experiencing the very same thing. Together.

ROSALIND: It is incredible.

WILKINS: Both watching.

ROSALIND: And when Hermione died, even though it was Leontes' fault, I felt for him. I truly did.

WILKINS: *Come, poor babe:*
I have heard, but not believed–

ROSALIND AND WILKINS: *The spirits o' the dead*
May walk again.

WILKINS: And they do. I love that Hermione wasn't really dead. That she comes back.

ROSALIND: *(Sympathetically.)* No, Maurice. She doesn't. Not really.

WILKINS: Of course she does.

ROSALIND: No.

WILKINS: Then how do you explain the statue coming to life?

ROSALIND: Hope. They all project it. Leontes projects life where there is none, so he can be forgiven.

WILKINS: But don't you think he deserves to be forgiven?

ROSALIND: Do I forgive myself?

WILKINS: What? For what?

Beat.

ROSALIND: You know…I think there must come a point in life when you realize you *can't* begin again. That you've made the decisions you've made and then you live with them or you spend your whole life in regret.

WILKINS: And I have spent my whole life in regret.

Beat.

ROSALIND: *(Smiling sadly.)* Well then perhaps we should have seen the play together.

Or gone to lunch.

WILKINS: Would that have changed things?

Long beat. She looks at him, decides to say something else.

ROSALIND: It's strange, you know. That I can't remember who played Hermione.

WILKINS: No…I can't either. Not for the life of me.

ROSALIND: She simply didn't stand out, I suppose.

(With less conviction.) And that's that.

The lights slowly fade.

By the same author

Anna Ziegler: Plays One

A Delicate Ship / Boy / The Last Match / Photograph 51

9781783193158

Actually

9781786823083